# THE WHOLE
# ART OF DRESS

## A Gentleman's
## GUIDE to APPAREL

FRONTISPIECE.

# THE WHOLE ART OF DRESS!

OR,

The Road to Elegance and Fashion,

AT THE

## ENORMOUS SAVING OF THIRTY PER CENT!!!

### BEING A TREATISE

UPON THAT ESSENTIAL AND MUCH-CULTIVATED REQUISITE
OF THE PRESENT DAY,

### GENTLEMEN'S COSTUME;

Explaining, and clearly defining, by a Series of

### BEAUTIFULLY ENGRAVED ILLUSTRATIONS,

The most becoming Assortment of Colours, and Style of Dress and
Undress, in all their varieties; suited to different Ages and
Complexions, so as to render the Human Figure most
Symmetrical and Imposing to the Eye.

ALSO, DIRECTIONS IN
THE PURCHASE OF ALL KINDS OF WEARING APPAREL:

Accompanied by
### HINTS FOR THE TOILETTE,

Containing a few valuable and original Recipes; likewise, some Advice
to the Improvement of Defects in the Person and Carriage.
Together with a Dissertation on Uniform in general,
and the Selection of Fancy Dress.

## BY A CAVALRY OFFICER.

BRITISH LIBRARY

This edition published 2018 by
The British Library
96 Euston Road
London NW1 2DB

ISBN 978 0 7123 5271 0

First published 1830

Cataloguing in Publication Data
A catalogue record for this publication
is available from the British Library

Designed by Samuel Clark,
By The Sky Design

Printed and bound in Malta by Gutenberg Press

# INDEX.

"A pleasing exterior is the first letter of recommendation."
—*Lord Chesterfield.*

# PREFACE.

The numerous advantages, with the importance resulting from an elegant personal appearance, are too generally known and appreciated throughout civilized Europe, to require much comment on here. The master-key alone, frequently, to the susceptible fancy of Beauty, its fascinating influence, alike commands admiration at the Bar, the Senate, or the Camp, as well as in the more retired shades of humble life.

It is only to be lamented, that the enormous charges usually incident to a desirable appearance, preclude many of limited incomes from enjoying it, while it brings down distress upon others. For I think it will almost invariably be found, that the first embarrassment young men—more especially our city youth with small salaries—bring upon themselves, is through endeavouring to support a fashionable exterior in the usually extensive method; hence in time results inability to pay, with the certain after consequences of arrest, and, with sorrow I pen it, too frequently entire ruin.

To obviate these too frequent occurrences—felt severely by so many entitled by birth and education to display that exterior of which youth is so susceptible—is the purpose of the present little volume, which is submitted to the eyes of a discerning Public, with the confident assurance that it will be found neither useless nor uninstructive; but, on the contrary, it is hoped, confer a benefit upon those disposed to follow its behests. They are simply laid down, pointed out with accuracy, and will receive confirmation in every respect by the proof of practice.

With regard to myself, and my ability for the present undertaking—entering the army

very young, with but a trifling annuity, independent of my pay as a subaltern of horse, few
men have been more obliged to make dress and
appearance altogether their study, than I have
with a limited finance. Consequently there are,
perhaps, equally few who, even after spending,
like myself, the greater part of a lifetime on
service, amid all the varied scenes and vicis-
situdes of a soldier's life at home and abroad,
are more capable, from *experience*, of writing
on economy, as relates to the pleasing exterior
of fashionable dress.

But previous to proceeding further, I should
wish those at all disposed towards consulting
this little, and I trust efficacious oracle, will
endeavour to eradicate from their minds a
rank and unwholesome weed, too frequently
obscuring and usurping an undue force in the
intellect. I mean that bane to the success of
many an excellent undertaking, *prejudice!*
There are many people, otherwise, perhaps,
very liberal and sensible in their ideas, devoutly
impregnated with the firm belief, that nothing
can be good that is *cheap*, and that to have

things excellent an immense price must needs be paid*—that there are but four tradesmen in the world capable of dressing a man to the height of perfection. Absurdity and nonsense; all chimeras: this may be believed in by the indolent, and luxurious rich, for they have the means of throwing money away, and can afford to be fools: but this by no means should be the criterion for men of small incomes; for having west-end tailors, with the supply of fashions at the usual enormous rate under those circumstances, is to incur the evils previously enumerated, and that too without occasion, as my future pages shall make manifest.

Though how to array the person to the best and most becoming advantage at the least possible expense, is the chief design of the following work, I have likewise deemed it requisite to allude to the toilette, which in itself is inseparably connected with the appearance, and therefore illustrative of my undertaking; but more especially I have thought proper to treat of the figure and carriage, without attention to which no dress can be becoming.

*The following little anecdote, which occurred when I was quartered with a detachment of my regiment in the north of England, is laughably illustrative of this fact. I was prevailed upon one day, by a friend possessed of more money than *taste*, as the sequel will show, to accompany him, as he was going to purchase a pipe of wine, of which commodity he considered himself a very efficient judge. Arrived at the merchant's, with the sagest and gravest face in the world, he tasted sample after sample, of the best and most expensive wines in the cellars, but none of them were sufficiently good for his palate. One wanted flavour, another body, and so on, as smacking his lips he successively gave the most knowing shakes of his head, plainly intimating he was not to be misled in his choice. "Have you no better? no dearer?" was his constant demand. At length the merchant placed in his hands, what he informed him was a specimen of the best wine in his cellars, at the same time, naming a moderate price. My friend differed with me "too thin," for him—"too much acid—not sufficiently rich," &c. He was departing, when the obsequious merchant begged his pardon—he had forgotten—he had in his possession one pipe of unusually fine old port, it was very dear, and he could not afford to sell it for less than—and he named an immense price. My friend's countenance brightened up as he spoke; he tasted; was in ecstasies at the vintage—"the very thing—something like wine *that*," and immediately ordered the pipe to be sent in. Was it the wine that influenced his choice? No! Was it the price? Yes! Because it was *dear*, and dear indeed it was, for the circumstance afterwards got known, through the merchant's foreman, that he had purchased the same wine he had previously rejected, paying just double the value.—So much for prejudice—I pray you avoid it!

I cannot but be aware that there will not be wanting those, who at the first sight of my title-page may imagine my pen verging in the promotion and defence of dandyism. Far from it! while I would uphold a smart and manly exterior, I repel, with merited contempt, the effeminate foppery of the other; and on perusal it will be found that the rules and advice here laid down as well apply to the old as young. As dress is a word in general signification, and comprehending in particular no immediate costume, I have thought fit to extend my original design to the wearing of uniform, and the lighter and more fanciful department of stage and masquerade dress; of which, from a residence abroad, more particularly in Italy, experience and observation enable me to speak with useful advice and directions in the selection, purchase, or hire of the same.

And now I have only to observe, I have spared neither trouble nor study, by consulting the few scanty authorities extant upon my subject, so that I may render the present little volume a work of general reference as regards dress and appearance. But ere I take my leave of the reader, with these few preliminary remarks, I cannot but seize this opportunity of returning my most cordial thanks to one or two friends, for much valuable information, and many very excellent hints, which they will perceive to my utmost I have endeavoured to profit by.

THE AUTHOR.

I cannot but be aware that there will not be wanting those who at the first sight of my Title Page may imagine my pen verging in the promotion and defence of Dandyism. Far from it!—while I would uphold a smart and manly exterior, I repel, with merited contempt, the effeminate foppery of the other; and, on perusal, it will be found that the rules and advice here laid down as well apply to the old as young.
—*Vide Preface.*

# THE WHOLE ART OF DRESS.

## CHAPTER I.

As the progress of civilization has gradually
increased in each successive age, dress, that
essential study to appearance, seems to have
undergone no slight revolution in each succeed-
ing century; and, if our limits but permitted,
we could show up a laughable and whimsical
contrast in the various fashions—that each has
had its "little brief authority," and then sunk
into the stream of time: many to rise no more.
And, now, as we look back upon past centuries,
and can scarce repress our laughter at many

of the absurd fancies in costumes our ances-
tors wore with such dignified gravity, inspiring
respect around them, it is accompanied by the
moralizing reflection that our present beloved
fashions, equally in their turn, and perhaps with
more justice, may become subjects of wonder
and mirth to our future descendants. So much
for the force and contrast of custom.

Of the vast estimation and consequence,
however, that have been, and are attached by
all orders of people, in all ages and in all coun-
tries, to appearance, there can be no doubt—the
outward man being but too frequently considered a specimen of the interior—of mental and
moral excellence; and, perhaps, alone, from
the frequent difference of these attributes of
humanity, arises that sage and homely proverb
"appearances are deceitful."

Though excellence of exterior is so universally
commended, and its magic influence acknowledged; though so much admired and desired by
every one, it is by no means generally known
how much depends upon, and can be effected
by art, towards arriving at this desideratum.

I have known some young men who, perhaps, labouring under very ordinary countenances and figures, have conceived themselves slighted in company by beauty, and have, through excess of sensibility, abandoned themselves to despondency; and, becoming morose and gloomy, have been lost to those little endearments of society that tend to lighten our path through life.

On the contrary, too, I have been frequently forced to observe others, similarly unfavoured in the exterior of formation by dame Nature, boldly have recourse to the mazes of art for redemption, and present a truly wonderfully improved appearance; so much so, that by following the dictates of taste and judgment in dress, and the arrangement of the toilette, by some they have actually been pronounced handsome.

Though it has been generally asserted by the learned, and indeed by writers in common, that great attention to outward seeming bespeaks great want of intellect, this, I infer, in some degree, is neither more nor less than a reason or apology submitted to the world for their own probable *professional* insufficiency in that respect. As this refers to the present age, at least, it must certainly universally be admitted to be an error; for we have only to look back to that great luminary of the present century, the immortal Byron, than whom, perhaps, no man ever more consulted or studied appearance, even in its most trifling minutiæ, than he did. I by no means instance a solitary exception: witness Moore, Campbell, and Southey, with twenty others celebrated for their attainments in literature; and, to go a little further back, the great little Pope himself, who actually wore *stays*—an uncommon proof of dandyism in those days. Therefore, it may be truly said, that attention to the exterior is by no means incompatible with the highest order of mental excellence and attainment.

Again, there is another charge frequently applied, as regards consulting dress and the mirror—this word, in general misapplication, is puppyism! Now I apprehend that, unlike dandyism, the application of this is, or ought

to be, to the mind exclusively, and not the face
or figure, against which it generally is levelled.
Puppyism, in *reality*, is nothing more than
conceit, centred in the *mind* from the knowledge, or fancied knowledge, of possessing
advantages by no means in common. It may,
with truth, in its literal and general meaning,
without any perversion of its sense, be far more
properly applied to a conceited clergyman or
quaker, than a *beau*, as polite phraseology goes;
only, indeed, that lawless tyrant custom has
substituted "pedantic"—a word that relates only
to learning in its proper stead.

In itself, dress, over the habitable globe, has
ever been, and is, regulated by *habit* in a great
degree more or less, except in civilized Europe,
where that staid regulator is fast loosing itself,
getting superseded by a *turn-coat whirligig
maniac*, yclept Fashion, that is always chang-
ing and running into extremes, being scarcely
ever detected in one form before it is out of it.
The idol of Paris and London, and the sun
of the western hemisphere: in the metropolis it is this that entirely governs the dressing

department, from the first-rate exquisite
of nobility, who has the last new superb cut
from Stultz's, down to the shop-swell in the
east "vot has the last reg'lar *bang-up-go*" from
the Borough.

Of fashion, in the following portion of
this treatise, it is my intention to speak generally, but by no means to enter into its long
and tiresome minutiæ, but only chiefly to
notice such portions of it as are calculated
to display to advantage the *tout ensemble*.
Indeed it would not only be ephemeral and
useless, but occupy that space dedicated to more
important matter. For those of our readers,
if any such perchance there be, desirous of following the very height of the ton, they have
only to take in a monthly periodical, entitled
*Bell's Gentlemen's Fashions*.

And now to enter on the system of economy
which I so much recommend to the middling
orders of society, to whom these pages are more
particularly addressed: it is nothing more, in
fact, than being your own agent. How you
may with the greatest ease become so, and the

advantages arising from it, I shall proceed to show, with all the requisite knowledge that should be attached thereto.

That most persons pay actually twice the sum that is requisite for clothing, I think I can fairly prove in the following just estimates. The following prices will be found, on an average, at respectable shops:

## TAILORS' PRICES,

### MADE TO ORDER.

|  | £ | s. | d. |
|---|---|---|---|
| Best superfine black or blue dress Coat | 4 | 0 | 0 |
| Ditto, ditto, ditto, Trowsers | 2 | 2 | 0 |
| Ditto, ditto, kerseymere Waistcoat | 1 | 1 | 0 |
|  | £ 7 | 3 | 0 |

Now for reformation. On proceeding to a draper's, such as I have named in the list at the end of this article, the following will be found the price of cloth, where likewise it can be made up, if so desired, or at a job tailor's. The estimate, at its dearest rate, is as follows:

|  | £ | s. | d. |
|---|---|---|---|
| The very best superfine black or blue cloth, at 1*l*. 1*s*. per yard, three yards | 3 | 3 | 0 |
| Making up into a suit | 1 | 5 | 0 |
|  | £ 4 | 8 | 0 |

Thus, deducting 4*l*. 8*s*. from 7*l*. 3*s*., there is a clear saving of 2*l*. 15*s*. on the suit, being about forty per cent: and, as regards the quality and make altogether of the clothes thus purchased, with such an immense saving, in nine cases out of ten, I am convinced they are

infinitely superior, and these are my reasons:—
In the first place, purchasing the cloth at a
wholesale and highly respectable shop, you
may always be certain of having it of the very
first quality, *spic span* new, and not soiled
and filled with dust, as is frequently the case
when it comes out of a tailor's shop, from
lying exposed in the window. In the next place,
as regards the making of the cloth up, it is
by no means generally known that the
job or journeymen tailors you employ on
this occasion, are the very men that would
have done the work, had you given the order
to a master-tailor; so that not the slightest
doubts need be entertained of any deficiency
in the cutting and sewing: on the contrary,
I always think they are done better; for it is
only natural to suppose that a man takes a
greater pride, consequently a greater care, in
working upon his own account, and is much
more actuated by a desire to give satisfaction,
and secure patronage, than when employed
by a master over him: neither, likewise, has
he occasion, having plenty of cloth, to resort

to those petty expedients of cutting, clipping, and joining to save cloth, that is invariably done by tailors when making clothes.

One thing indeed in pursuing this plan is requisite, provided you are no judge of cloth yourself, which in a very short time you soon may be; you should always get some one who is, that you may not be imposed upon in some strange shop. For instance, the man you employ, for a couple of shillings or so, will attend, and by whose advice you will be guided as regards the quality of the article; taking care, however, not to have above the requisite quantity, for what may chance to be left they never return, considering it as a perquisite. As I have previously however said, three yards will be found about the average quantity.

As London, at the present period, abounds with mercenary and unprincipled tradesmen, where the unguarded novice is too frequently taken advantage of, for the greater security of my readers in this respect, I have thought fit to select two tradesmen in each department of this work, (from the east and west of the

metropolis,) in whom, from their high respect-
ability, and the noted cheapness of their shops,
the utmost reliance may be placed. But of
advice in selection and purchase I shall speak
hereafter; at present I shall commence to
analyze the different articles of dress coming
under the denomination of a suit.

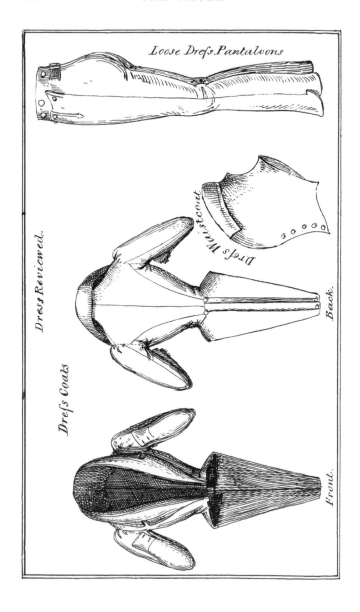

*Loose Dress Pantaloons*

*Dress Waistcoat*

*Dress Reviewed.*

*Dress Coats*

*Back.*

*Front.*

# CHAPTER II.

―――――

## COATS.

THESE are generally considered the *sine qua non* of dress, a good coat (or rather coatee, as it is now more properly called, lappels not being worn) diffusing the halo of its splendour over the rest of the person, and making the trousers and waistcoat, however faded, participate in its holiday newness. And this it most certainly does to a certain extent, as it is, without doubt, by far the most important in comparison with the rest of the dress, both as regards expense and difficulty of make. In fact the greatest care and attention should be bestowed in giving directions in this most consequential feature of male attire; as the appearance of the neck, shoulders, chest, and waist, nay, the whole person itself, depends exclusively upon its make.

As there never should be a wrinkle observable in a coat, there is a very excellent plan I most earnestly recommend to the attention of the reader, to ensure the most perfect fit *possible*. I myself have followed it with the greatest success. When you have, or can get a coat to fit you, without at all creasing (which may easily be done by having each successive coat made without the faults of its predecessor) have all the others cut *precisely* by it, with the exception of the prevailing fashion. Though there may be found occasion to alter or vary the collar or tail from this pattern, the body of it (the chief requisite) will never require any altering whatever. By these means, it is in the power of every one to ensure the most admirable fit, and it also cannot but give greater confidence, in giving the cloth out to make to a stranger workman, when you know he has an exact pattern to go by.

The three chief beauties requisite in the appearance of a coat, in the present day, consist in colour, gloss, and make. The former should be invariably dark, as black, blue, dark browns, and greens; except, indeed, in the heat of summer, when a very light brown is worn, which, on account of its not displaying the dust that accumulates, looks very well. Gilt buttons are only worn with blue. The gloss of a coat, though it be very handsome, and the harbinger of newness, should never be too satiny, if I may be allowed the term: in the first place, it is perhaps taken for, or at least reminds one of the stuff shopmen's coats are composed of; in the next, it is always unserviceable, as it spots with the rain; and last, not least, the best cloths are never remarkable for this qualification. With regard to that essential, the *cut*, a coat should always sit easy and close to the shoulders, and close in at the back, the skirts hanging smoothly, without the slightest crumple. By the way (a word in the ear of the Exquisite), a small roll of lead, weighing about two ounces, sewed in the interior of each pocket, greatly facilitates this, and likewise from the gentle stress improves the sit in the back.

The front of a dress coat should be so made, that the chest should look very broad and prominent. The present fashion is for the sides to be extended back and look like a continuation of the collar, which should be wide and sloping, so as nearly to obscure the sight of the buttons. These should be of silk, plain, and very small.

A dress coat should never be made to button. It should, if any thing, be even too small to meet across the waist and chest, so that it may sit open and display the waistcoat, shirt, and cravat to the utmost advantage. Black and blue are the only full-dress colours: night will not allow a dark green to be discriminated from them. Surtout-coats, which are almost all made double-breasted, are nearly the only, or at least the chief undress wear of fashionables westward and eastward. The attention should be most directed in the make of these (which, I think, only look well buttoned up close to the throat) to the sit of the skirts, which should be made proportionably full to the closeness of the fit round the waist. This kind of coat should always, to look well, be rather thickly and tastefully padded in front. A velvet collar, too, is becoming. Black, blue, and olive are, I think, nearly the only colours worn. A small *fly*, as it is called, is a very excellent invention in these coats, as it enables you to pull the waist into a very small dimension, without fear of bursting the button-holes, which are entirely relieved from pressure by it. In buttoning up, however, the last button should never be used. It makes the coat sit more out at the hips.

## WAISTCOATS.

This portion of dress has become very gay latterly, the richest and most brilliant coloured velvets and silks, sprigged and shot, having superseded both kerseymere and toilenettes, in a very great degree: so much so, that cloth waistcoats are never seen worn by any but a few professional men. The collars that are now worn to them are short and lap over, as in a double-breasted waistcoat, and when the waist-coat is composed of silk, are generally made of velvet, black or blue.

The make of a waistcoat is of consequence, as it affects, in open dress, both the appearance of the chest and waist—the two portions upon which the figure wholly hangs. On the former it should sit round, sloping and rather full, round the latter very close.

For my own individual taste, notwithstanding the superb richness of the materials chiefly used now in this department, by those who make dress at all a study, I can conceive nothing more beautiful than spotless white or bright yellow kerseymere for full dress, with buttons of the same; the more especially so when worn with a velvet stock. In full dress, never make use of more than three buttons. In winter, for general wear, the double-breasted look very handsome, though, like all other portions of dress, they should never be worn when so much out of general fashion as to look singular.

## PANTALOONS.

Perhaps, indeed, there is no portion of dress that of late years has claimed more attention from the bloods of fashion, than trousers or pantaloons. Whether it be considered that the lamentable deficiency, too frequently perceptible in their *understandings*, claims extra notice I know not, but so it is, that the shape of the trousers seems as indispensable as that of the coat now. But still the fashions, as may be remarked, are various, tight-kneed and full being worn almost indiscriminately. The make, too, has undergone a general change; the trousers buttoning down the front have rendered nugatory the use of flaps. Though this certainly I think an improvement, the fashion is by no means new, but only an old one revived.

The fashion of raised seams down the side seems now almost generally discarded; this, with the large fall which accompanies the make of trousers, small legged or full, are copied decidedly, with many other etcæteras, from the army, who, considering the long peace, have certainly been very popular in dress. Nothing can more improve the look and fit of trousers than double straps; these, with very full cossack-trowsers, are more indispensably requisite when the legs are particularly crooked or ill-formed. The appearance of stature, too, is immensely affected by pantaloons, but of this I purpose speaking under a different head.

Regarding tight pantaloons in full dress, though certainly the most proper and becoming in every point of view, yet I would by no means advise any of my readers to assume these without they have at least tolerably good legs. Unless, indeed, they particularly choose to have recourse to art to supply the defects of a crooked or a thin leg; in which cases a slight degree of stuffing is absolutely requisite, but the greatest care and circumspection should be used. The finest double-milled black kersey mere should compose them.

*Names and Addresses of Woollen-Drapers.*

Wm. Bourne and Co. 59, Coleman-street,
and 48, Regent-street.
Wm. Carpenter, 37, Leadenhall-street.

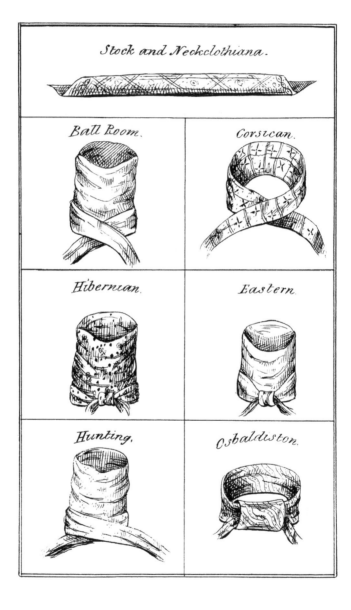

Stock and Neckclothiana.

Ball Room.

Corsican.

Hibernian.

Eastern.

Hunting.

Osbaldiston.

# CHAPTER III.

CRAVATIANA.

## OF STOCKS AND NECKCLOTHS.

I SHALL now proceed to note and comment upon a portion of dress, in the selection and method of wearing which taste and neatness is pre-eminently to be distinguished; more particularly in full costume. First I shall treat of Stocks, which, though assuming a variety of forms, and shaped for the sake of perspicuity, I have distinguished only under their three general heads, the Royal George or Full Dress, the Plain Beau, and the Military.

The origin of stocks is very ancient, though for the last half-century they have been worn almost exclusively by the army, navy, and marines, until first revived into public notice by his late Majesty, in the year 1822, when they immediately became an universal fashion.

Though at first viewed with a prejudiced and jealous eye by friends of the old school, after some opposition from the *petits maîtres* tribe, they at length found their way into the opera and ball-room, and became a portion of full-dress costume. But this has only occurred since his Majesty was pleased to display one at Drury-lane theatre, composed of velvet and satin, from whence the present full-dress stock takes its name. Habit still, however, in some degree, reflects upon stocks for evening costume, and the adoption, though increasing, is by no means at present popular among the ton. I now proceed to describe the three fashions I have classed them under.

## THE ROYAL GEORGE,

or Full Dress. This stock, the shape of which is left in a great degree to the wearer's pleasure, is composed of the richest black Genoa velvet and satin, the latter of which, sloping down each side of the velvet, terminates in the centre with a very handsome tie, representing a small gordian knot, with short broad ends. From the beautiful and lively contrast, of the velvet and satin, this stock is peculiarly becoming to dark complexions, as nothing can afford a stronger relief than the deep sable of its exterior. His Majesty and his royal brothers were always remarkable for wearing them extremely high on the cheek, so that the sides came close under the ears, extending to the utmost verge of the chin. Though this certainly gives a very noble and fine effect to some countenances, the rage for it has passed away and is now deemed singular.

## THE PLAIN BOW

is nearly straight-sided, very pliant, and composed entirely of black silk, with a common bow in front. Though of an humble aspect beside its more haughty and aristocratical contemporaries, its appearance is unassuming and businesslike. Fashion decidedly *Oriental.*

## THE MILITARY

is remarkable for the plain stiff elegance of its form, which is composed of corded silk, edged with kid and lined with crimson; unlike the two former fashions it has no tie. The shape or stiffner should be made of a thick whity-brown leather, which is beaten into shape upon a proper block, it should then be of so unyielding a nature that no force of the neck can bend it. A good shape ought to bear new covering at least a dozen times. The *tout ensemble* of this fashion expresses plainness and dignity with neatness and *hauteur* in an infinite degree.

Of stocks in general, it may be observed, that
they are both handsome and economical, and
are not attended with half the trouble of cravats,
to which they become a pleasing change, more
especially so in dark or gloomy weather, when
light-coloured neckerchiefs have a very forlorn
appearance. Of course it need scarcely be said
that the military and plain beau should never be
assumed for full dress. A large sable-coloured
hook and eye, will be found an excellent and easy
substitute for a buckle behind, the arrangement
of which is frequently tiresome in the extreme.

With regard to Neckcloths, it is first indispensably necessary to premise, that previous
to putting into execution the fashions here
developed, the utmost attention should be paid
to their washing, bleaching, and starching;
the latter of which must generally be used in
such proportion as to stiffen the cloth to the
consistence of fine writing-paper. You may
then confidently make your first folds as in
the annexed plate; and then, with some slight
practice and care, may execute the following
ties at pleasure.

## BALL-ROOM.

This, perhaps, of all the following ties is, when
well executed, the most exquisite, and requires
the greatest practice. The cloth, of virgin white,
well starched, and folded to the proper depth,
should be made to sit easy and graceful upon
the neck, neither too tight nor loose, but with
a gentle pressure, curving inwards, from the
further extension of the chin, down the throat,
to the centre dent in the middle of the neck. This
should be the point for a slight dent, extending from under each ear, between which, more
immediately under the chin, there should be
another slight horizontal dent, just above the
former one. It has no tie; the ends, crossing each
other in broad folds in front, are secured to the
braces, or behind the back by means of a piece
of white tape. A brilliant brooch or pin is generally made use of to secure more effectually the
crossing, as well as to give an additional effect
to the neckcloth.

## THE CORSICAN,

or Napoleon, is most simple, but by no means inelegant, being nothing more than the neckcloth first placed on the back of the neck, brought round in front, and the ends crossed and fastened as in the preceding method.

This, like some of the ensuing fashions, when the cloth first comes from the back of the neck, is decidedly a summer wear, consequently most in vogue during June, July, and August, when it is delightfully cool and refreshing. A plain gold pin I recommend as the most handsome fasten for the front. Cerulean blue is the greatest favourite in this form; but this, with other colours that may be named, are only submitted to the reader's fancy.

## HIBERNIAN TIE.

This somewhat resembles the Ball-room, having a collateral dent coming from under each ear, but has only one horizontal. A small gordian knot is the fasten.—Colour, emerald green.

## EASTERN TIE.

This is very plain and neat. As there should not be the slightest crease visible, the greatest regard should be paid to having the cloth starched as stiffly as possible, without which it is very liable to bend. The sides should be quite straight and smooth, rather larger below than above, with a square knot in front.

White is almost the only colour exhibited in this fashion.

## HUNTING TIE.

This is most conspicuous for its height and tight-ness, and from the three creases on either side. Like the Corsican, the ends should be crossed and placed out of sight. A pin or brooch, bearing the representation of a fox's head, or some apposite emblem, is generally worn. Favourite colours, white, bright buff, or white spots on a blue ground.

## YANKEE TIE.

This tie is alone original, from the slight perpen-
dicular crease it has on either side of the chin. A
slight collateral dent should likewise be on each
side, but extending very little forwards, while the
folds of the cloth should come close under the
ears. A small, flat, gordian knot is the general
accompaniment to this, though I have known
them worn with the ends plainly crossed over
the breast.—Colour, light brimstone.

## OSBALDISTON TIE.

The fold of this should be extremely narrow,
for, like the Corsican, it is first brought from the
back of the neck, consequently chiefly intended
for summer. The tie, which is remarkable, is an
enormous barrel-knot, at least four inches in
length, and two deep. As this is entirely a fancy
tie, and chiefly worn by sporting characters, any
fancy colour is appropriate.

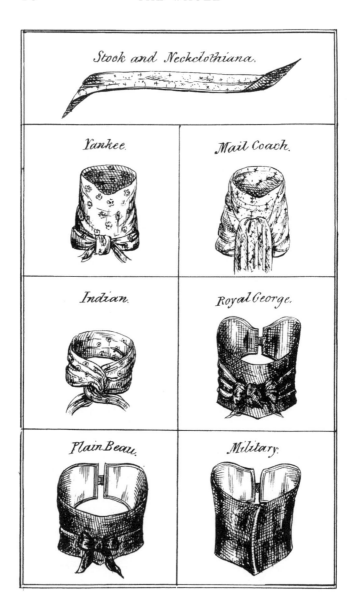

Stock and Neckclothiana.

Yankee.

Mail Coach.

Indian.

Royal George.

Plain Beau.

Military.

## MAIL-COACH TIE.

Two things are absolutely requisite, rather out of the common course, to form this tie, which should resemble a waterfall. In the first place, the cloth should be immensely large; in the second, it should have no starch. The tie is made by folding the cloth loosely round the neck, and fastening it with a common knot, over which the folds of the cloth should be spread, so as entirely to conceal it. This is the fashion most in repute among all *professional swell* drivers, from the mail-coach down to the hack or cabriolet.—Colour, generally white, but not unfrequently various, as suits the taste of its numerous wearers.

## INDIAN TIE.

Of all summer fashions, this, as its name may signify, is most in celebrity for its coolness, from being composed of the finest muslin. The ends are brought round the neck in front, linked transversely, and fastened. This, forming part of a nabob's costume, is worn generally under the tropics, for its uncommon ease and coolness, where I have seen it receive a very handsome and showy effect by the introduction of a ring as a slide, instead of the previous method.—Colours may be various, but always light—chequered are, perhaps, most adopted.

## HINTS

respecting the various departments and branches of neckcloth tying.

When a starched neckcloth is brought home from the wash, it will be immediately seen that one side is smooth and shining, the other more rough; this is occasioned by the one being ironed and the other not. I do it myself, and consequently recommend it to others, that the rough side should be worn outside during the day, but that on putting on a cloth for the evening, the smooth side should be the visible one.

After having folded the neckcloth, and made out the depth, &c., according to the wearer's taste, as I have previously said, the ends should first be folded as in the annexed engraving, the right-hand end of the cloth turned down, and, *vice versâ*, the end on the left, turned up. The second method, perhaps, is the most general in use, more particularly when a handsome knot is in request. This is effected by gradually deepening both sides of the cloth, commencing from that part touching the back of the neck to the extreme ends. These first folds, by the way, should invariably be ironed out by the washer, and never attempted by the common vulgar method of turning down with the hand.

The advantages of these rules will soon be discovered. It removes the awkward appearance caused by crossing the ends behind; the ends are also by this means brought forward in a smooth and uncrumpled state, and fit to make the knot. It also makes the neckcloth lay smooth and even behind, a thing which hitherto has been much neglected. The same care almost should be given to the back as the front part.

After the knot is made, take a piece of white tape and tie one end of it tight to one end of your neckcloth; then carry the tape under your arm, behind your back, under the other arm, and fasten it tightly to the other end of the neckcloth. The tape must *not* be visible. This way prevents the knot from flying up, which would thereby shorten the length of the cloth, and, in short, greatly injure its appearance. On putting on the neckcloth, take that part which is immediately under the ears with your thumb and finger, and pull it up till it reaches the ear, and contrive to make it maintain permanently that position. Nothing displays more *mauvais gout* than seeing a cloth forming a *straight* line from the chin to the ear.

Let the front part of the cloth be brought in a line with the extremity of the chin. Nothing gives a person more the appearance of a goose than to see a long part of the jaw and chin projecting over the neckcloth.

Great attention is requisite in starching of neckcloths, or they will turn yellowish, which gives the idea of having a dirty cloth on.

——————— Has he
Dislik'd your yellow starch?

*Fletcher.*

Starched neckcloths, independently of their superior look when compared with those which are not so, are also equally comfortable both in summer and winter.

The indentures of a starcher, and which, of course, when received inside, are projections, prevent the whole mass of linen touching the cheek. And in some (the Eastern for example) no part, except the extreme top and bottom edges, ever in any way touch the neck, which consequently leaves that part free and cool, thereby preventing in summer that overpowering heat occasioned by unstarched linen surrounding and closely clasping the neck on all sides.

In winter also it has its advantages; for the starch completely fills up all the smallest and most minute holes (I do not mean holes occasioned by wear, &c., but those which exist in all linen from the nature of its construction), and thereby effectually prevents the admission of the least portion of cold air.

Neckcloths should always (except those worn in the evening, and even *then* they may in ordinary be worn, if the ribs or chequers are not too visible), be made of ribbed or chequered materials, as it makes *far better* ties than when the stuff is plain. Muslin makes beautiful ties, especially for evenings. I had forgotten in its proper place to mention, that after the neck-cloth is finished, you should pass your finger along the upper ridge, in order to make it lay smooth, and look thin and neat. Of selection and purchase, &c., I shall treat after having described the other articles of dress coming under the denomination of linen.

# CHAPTER IV.

## ON LINEN.

### SHIRTS, POCKET-HANDKERCHIEFS, STOCKINGS, SOCKS, AND GLOVES.

---

### SHIRTS

ARE now the next article that comes into consideration under the present head. No inconsiderable degree of consequence has been attached to this necessary portion of dress by the fashionable leaders of late, as the present taste sufficiently displays. Though there is something very handsome and fanciful in the dress-shirts of the present day, they frequently seem to degenerate into tawdry. The bosoms or dress-fronts, as they are generally called, are invariably composed of lawn or worked cambric-muslin, which is puckered and furbelowed into a variety of ruffled shapes. Among these fancies, perhaps, a trellisworked lace front, on a pink ground, composed of silk or muslin, may be esteemed the most fascinating and killing in the eyes of *some*. For my own part, I think nothing can be more handsome, manly, and unassuming, than a plain cambric muslin frill. The wristbands, which should only be turned down the last thing on going to a ball or party, should be made of a considerable depth, collars the reverse; these I have seen frequently worked in the form of a string of flowers along the edge. I cannot say I approve of this kind of thing, there is too much *finesse* about it; fashions, too, are ephemeral, so that I would advise none of my readers to run into any of these extremes. In fact, there is a great advantage in always adopting the fashions three or four months behindhand, because you then assume, however ridiculous, what the public from habit are reconciled to, and may consequently pass through the streets without being annoyed by those sneers, laughs, and witticisms from the *canaille* which have previously been exhausted upon the first essayists.

As the wristbands, collars, and fronts are the only parts displayed in public, it is by no means absolutely requisite, it should be remembered, to have the body and sleeves composed of linen. On the contrary, fine India long cloth, while it saves an immense expense (one-third the price of linen), is infinitely superior, from the coolness and comfort of its wear. By this means the most elegantly-worked fronts may be worn, without any imputation of extravagance. Of the various-coloured fancy chequed shirts that at first assumed the name of aquatic, they may be termed both economical and fashionable, when selected and worn properly. The colours for common wear should never be too bright and conspicuous, nor should the collars or wristbands ever be displayed, except when on the water. As the tastes, perhaps, are so various in the choice of colours, I shall merely confine myself to recommending a very narrow stripe, at same breadth intervals of white; this may be chequered; blue is a favourite colour; glaring red is my aversion.

From being composed solely of cotton, these shirts are recommended generally by the faculty for summer wear, as they absorb the perspiration of the body, that being the reason why calico is always worn in India. Linen, it need scarce be remarked, does not possess their virtue in that respect, nor is it besides half so soft and comfortable to the skin. The advantages, indeed, which linen is said to possess over its contemporary, are in wear and the retention of its spotless hue to the last, while cotton turns slightly yellow; but experience has convinced me that very little difference, in reality, exists between them, when properly "got up," as the laundress' phraseology goes. And I would lay any wager, that a cotton shirt, if well made, might be worn twenty times in full dress, in the midst of women, and the fact never be discovered.

## POCKET-HANDKERCHIEFS.

This necessary and essential article of use, is generally composed of silk; cotton not being known among the middling ranks since the duty has been taken off silk. Excellent India silk handkerchiefs may now be bought for 5s. 6d. apiece, and are various as the patterns they exhibit, but, unlike British manufacture, are remarkable for keeping their dyes to the last. The silk, too, is the softest and most beautiful in the world, and is woven in two forms, plain and twilled, single and double, which latter, in fact, is most expensive, and considered most handsome. A rich crimson, with a variegated yellow border, is the *sine qua non* of India handkerchiefs, in my humble opinion. There are many ways of detecting false India silk; one is, to stretch the handkerchief tight over the top of a tumbler, and then strike the edge with a knife; if the silk be real India, such are its properties, that no knife, however sharp, will cut it. I have seen this successfully proved, over and over. Another ordeal an India should bear, is, to make it pass through a common-sized finger-ring. But I think myself that the eye and hand can never be deceived, the superiority of the real article being so evident over all imitating counterfeits. However rich and handsome India handkerchiefs may be, in ordinary wear, it should ever be recollected, that they have long ceased to hold a place in full costume; like that which is worn round the neck, it should be *le blanc virginale*, and is always composed of lawn or cambric muslin, frequently with a narrow strip of Brussels lace along the edges. This is a distinguishing corresponding mark of full dress, and has a very courtly and prepossessing appearance, more particularly among the fair ones.

## STOCKINGS AND SOCKS.

The latter of these, I believe, are only in general
wear among men, on account of the facility with
which they may be used, as well as to render
nugatory that horror of horrors, to persons possessing good legs—a garter. This is an order
the knights of fashion have universally forsworn.
The full-dress colours for socks are black and
grey silk, or gray and white-shotted, which latter,
last year, were all the rage, but are now getting
again superseded by the old standard colour,
black. White silk, some years back, was worn,
but is now only recognizable in uniform, with
white or yellow kerseymere smallclothes.

With respect to dress socks, as in other parts
of dress, it is at the option of the individual to
make a great saving by having the tops, toes,
and soles of cotton, and the fronts, where they
are seen, of silk.

For socks in ordinary, I would recommend
generally ribbed, unbleached cotton, or light
gray, both of which will be found serviceable
and economical.

GLOVES.

Nothing can give a more perfect finish to a handsome dress than the covering for the hands.
Though there are many different kinds worn,
those mostly in repute among the higher orders
are the Doe-skin, Kid and Berlin, which latter
was first introduced into fashion two seasons ago.

Doe-skin are chiefly adopted by the ton for
riding and driving; for either of which, from
their extreme softness, warmth, and thickness, they are very admirably contrived. Kid
of all materials is, without exception, the most
beautiful, and sits best on the hand, from its
exceeding pliability (when good); compressing
the hand with a gentle pressure, like a second
natural skin over the first. Buff, or white kid,
should alone be assumed for full dress.

We now come to the Berlin. These, looking
equally as well as Doe-skin or Woodstock,
I would particularly recommend to notice,
for the great economy attending their wear.
Gray and white are the most desirable colours.
These gloves are made of a kind of strong

cotton, which, while it should possess great strength, should be very thin and neat. The great advantage derived from their use (an advantage no other kind possesses), is their bearing washing the same as linen, which, when their texture is good, they will at least sustain twenty times, without showing any symptoms of wear. Great care, however, ought to be taken in their cleansing; and when boiled with a little pearlash, it will be found an excellent thing for producing a snowy whiteness that nothing can surpass.

Of the purchase of linen made up, or unmade, I shall say but little; it being a subject upon which the ladies alone (excepting drapers) are to be considered conversant, and to them I beg to refer my friendly readers on this important occasion. I shall merely content myself with observing, that too great a circumspection cannot be used in seeing that linen and calico are not dressed up with lime and other things, which at first gives it a very prepossessing appearance until washed, when the cheat is discovered. But this is a liability the reader need have no fear of incurring at the places I have named—the cheapest in London—for the sale of this department, where every facility and attention will be paid to the purchaser.

*Names and Addresses of Hosiers.*

Wm. Pitt, No. 125, Strand.
Elleman and Haggitts, No. 23, Poultry.

# CHAPTER V.

## ON HATS.

### THEIR FASHION AND MAKE, &C.

Iт is almost impossible to be conceived, by a person inexperienced in dress, the immense influence exclusively this department of dress has over the countenance and figure in regard to shape and method of wear. It affects both the appearances of age and stature, sobriety and rakishness in the individual. Indeed it forms a matter of amusement to observe the different styles men in the present period have of wearing their hats; and, if a general view of a man's character is any way to be guessed at by any portion of his dress, it certainly must be this, as the following common instances, in some degree, may show.

The Aylesbury.    The Turf.    The Oxonian.

The Collegian.    The Tilbury.    The Anglesea.

Caps.

The hat *à la militaire*, cocked fiercely on one side, intending doubtless to represent outwardly that recklessness and resolution which the wearer, perhaps, by no way inwardly feels.

Then there is the slouched broad hat, generally adopted by the aged and unfortunate to hide the countenance from the sight of former acquaintance that long affliction has perhaps rendered unnecessary. This wear, too, is very frequently used by town characters of a suspicious cast, who have a marvellous aptitude, when certain eyes chance to glance on them, to scamper down the first alley at hand.

Next comes the man-of-business fashion, the hat being thrust carelessly on the back of the head, as though the tenant within were too much occupied with its own communings to care for the exterior.

Lastly, of those I shall notice comes the fop; his forehead receiving the greater portion of his "het," which is perched with the most *exquisite* adjustment on the "precise tip-top of his head," as though fearful a too closer intimacy would crumple the ringlets of hair that adorn his countenance.

In fact it may, I think, truly be said, there are no bumps in phrenology on the *head* so indicative of the interior as simply the method of wearing a hat. As regards, too, stature and age, the most wonderful changes in appearance can be effected by a hat. A very high and small crowned hat, with a narrow round rim (as the Tilbury) contrasted with a broad, wide crown and rim (as the Turf), will make a man, if about forty, look about ten or eleven years younger, and an inch or two taller. Now this is a fact that by no means is generally known; but I have frequently seen the deception practised, and know it to be so, it merely requiring the experiment to force conviction of its truth beyond all doubt.

Perhaps there is no article of dress possessed of so many reigning fashions as hats, which have chiefly received their names from the different persons who have patronised their various shapes. Among the many fashions before me at present, I shall select only six as

originals, which are in general wear. These are
the Oxonian, Turf, Aylesbury, Anglesea, Tilbury,
and Collegian.

From these I select the Aylesbury for its neat
and gentlemanlike shape, which, together with
the Anglesea, are becoming to oval countenances. Hats with round rims should ever be
worn for setting off this kind of face.

For faces indeed that are round or short, it
will be found, by consulting the mirror, that the
Tilbury will be found most becoming, as it is
turned up at the sides. The materials that hats
are composed of in England are either beaver
or silk, or sometimes the two together.

Beaver, until latterly, has been almost solely
worn among the nobility and gentry; a silk hat
(if known) only recalling a low mechanic to the
ideas of the former upon the subject. Now the
reason why so great a preference has always
been given by the *fashionables* to beaver, while
silk has been abominated, as well as their rela-
tive properties, I intend slightly expatiating
on. Of beaver, the chief and essential properties that it is said to have had over silk was,

its extreme lightness and pliability, and I may say shape; for until very lately silk hats have been taken little notice of by the middling orders, there was ever a vast distinction made in this last particular. Silk hats were invariably made large-crowned, when the fashion was for small; so that those who might have been partial to silk, could not obtain a fashionable shape. This in fact seemed premeditated among the manufacturers to enhance the prices of beaver. This, however, has been since remedied, I am happy to say, for the sake of economy and fashion; and to such perfection are silk hats now manufactured, at half the price of beaver, that they may be obtained nearly as light, and quite as elegant in shape and gloss, and above all, far more durable. In fact, while scarcely to be distinguished from each other, there is an advantage that silk hats will ever possess over beaver, which is, that the gloss on silk, though it wear at the sides, which should be double-edged, will continue to the last, while beaver turns quite brown, and looks very shabby.

The only advantage which beaver, in its turn, possesses over silk, is its elastic property, so that it runs scarcely any risk in getting bent or broken, as common manufactured silk hats. For this purpose, to extend a similar benefit to silk, or, to couple their respective advantages, silk is frequently used for covering beaver shapes, which, from their cheapness, I strongly recommend.

Black, white, and copper, are the only colours of hats, the two latter being only worn during the summer months. To countenances of a lively expression, whether fair or dark, white hats have a very genteel and handsome appearance; that is, with a certain style of dress, for, in assuming them, attention to colours is absolutely requisite. No colour sorts so well with a *chapeau blanc* as green, next blue, and brown; both should be of a lightish hue; but beware of black. If this be fancy, it is one which, I am inclined to think, close observation should render general. Clothes, too, should be invariably good when a white hat is assumed.

The great advantage, in point of comfort, in wearing white hats, is their coolness, contrasted with black, the copperas in the dye of the latter having a very powerful influence in attracting the rays of the sun. For this reason, I have a great objection to the copper-coloured, that in fact are dyed with the mineral from whence they are named, on which account they are unhealthy in the extreme—at the same time, I think, they have no redeeming qualities, their hue being neither one thing nor the other, but an indifferent sort of go-between. Perhaps some of my readers, in wearing this description of hat beneath a burning sun, may have complained of headach. On reading the foregoing, the reader, I trust, will know what to ascribe it to. In wearing one of these hats—that I am well convinced are very pernicious from their poisonous dye—during a hot summer-season, I think the probable chance would be greatly in favour of its causing a brain fever.

After all, however, that may be said on the subject, black hats are decidedly, when taken in a general view, the most becoming and

fashionable, June, July, and August excepted,
when light colours of all descriptions of clothing
are generally adopted for the sake of coolness.

However excellent the rest of an individual's
dress may be, nothing diminishes its bright-
ness more, and throws a shade over the whole
person, than a hat when it is old. Wear any
portion of dress faded but this, as you value the
look of your face and appearance in general.
Avoid as infectious, in the present state of
fashion, broad crowns and broad brims; for a
handsome shape with a new hat is quite indispensable, and which, by giving orders to the
shopman, may always be obtained. And yet
we have but to take a short walk, either west
or eastwards, to have our risibility provoked
at the "crude and undigested" shapes one is
fated to meet with, in those, perhaps, too, who
would fain be thought masters of the most noble
art of dress—an art, be it said and heard with
veneration, that gradually, in its various degrees
of civilization throughout the world, is one of
the grand outward distinctions between the
untaught savage and the European.

As I have previously observed, an appropriate shaping should always distinguish a hat with those who in any way regard appearance;—this may be effected by any one with a little trouble. In improving then the form of a hat, old or new, silk or beaver, you have only to hold the rim (where the projected alteration can only be made) to the fire, until the substance of which the hat is composed gets warm and soft; in which state the rim should be hastily brushed, to prevent the beaver or silk spoiling, when you may proceed to shape with the finger and thumb—the method adopted by all hatters. Beaver is far the most pliable, and easily turned; however, you should keep supporting up the shape you intend, with the hand, until the hat cools, when it becomes durable. If the hat be silk that undergoes this operation, great care should be taken to prevent the silk rising, by constant application of the hand, the silk being only held by a kind of glue:—the hat should previously undergo a good brushing. Dust is the destruction of all hats. Nothing preserves a hat more from dissolution than a careful rub with a soft brush;—when the hat be new indeed, a silk handkerchief may be used.

Having now expended my remarks upon hats I turn to caps. Independent of the united service of Great Britain, these seem of late years to have fallen entirely into disuse, except among boys and the lower orders generally. These latter gentry I have been forced to observe with disgust, wearing navy and army regulation at times, with the utmost *nonchalance*, as though perfectly ignorant of, or accustomed to, the honour they were sullying. More especially the last winter, it was really amusing to perceive groups of low apprentice-lads with cloaks and naval caps, with chin-pieces down, shuffling about in divers holiday-places, to the utmost indignation, doubtless, of the youthful aspirants in either gallant service. For the above reason it has grown almost degrading to wear a cap in public, however comfortable or convenient at times. In archery-meetings and shooting-parties, however, they are commonly worn by the higher orders of society, and under such circumstances are, beyond all doubt, much more unencumbering and pleasant than hats.

Caps are manufactured in an immense variety of shapes: that which I think is the handsomest and most becoming is composed entirely of cloth, without any front or stiff shape, which should be tied by a broad ribbon of the same colour as the cap; this is mostly made of blue, green, or brown cloth; blue I think the most preferable colour, which looks very well with the broad ends of the ribbon hanging down the left cheek. This fashion, independent of the red and white chequer, is decidedly Scotch fashion, and is worn in undress by the 72nd and other Highland regiments. Its appearance is certainly singularly simple, martial, and elegant. Of hats or caps, in common, to conclude, I would strongly inculcate into my reader's mind, that nothing should be worn *outré*, or in any way conspicuous out of the common course of that station in life or profession, in which he may move. Undue assumption in dress, it may be relied on, never fails to meet with contempt in society, where, in fact, it can only expose the party to a very just and proper censure.

*Names and Addresses of Hatters.*

R. Lloyd, No. 71, Strand, late of Newgate-street.
Barber and Son, No. 19, Sweetings-alley, Cornhill.

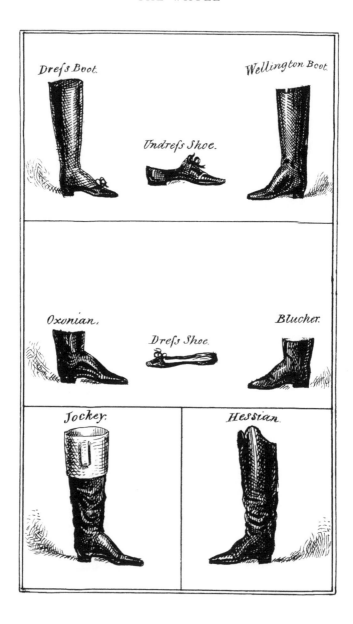

# CHAPTER VI.

---

## ON BOOTS AND SHOES.

### THEIR VARIOUS KINDS AND FASHIONS, &C.

As in China, the greatest attention is displayed to the feet in the fashionable world; their importance vying with any other portion of the figure. Indeed to such an excess have I seen this carried, that frequently in company I have heard the chief beauties singled out among good-looking individuals, were their feet; because, perhaps, they have been rather small and cased in a neat pump. These are *low* ideas it must be confessed, reversing with a verity the old quotation, "from head to foot!"

Under the denomination of boots and shoes comes a variety of kinds, which I shall name and speak of in the separate and individual qualities and advantages they relatively possess; while for the better elucidation of my meaning, when the reader should be in any doubt, a reference to the annexed plate will be only necessary. First and foremost, under the appellation of boots comes Hessian, then Top, Wellington, Collegian, and Blucher or "high-lows," as they are vulgarly called.

## THE HESSIAN

is a boot only worn with tight pantaloons, a fashion entirely copied from the military, and is very common in Germany and France, where it generally forms a part of equipment in the cavalry. Of late years, however, this kind of boot has been introduced among our own military horse. The fashions, with respect to the boot have been very capricious, leaving it neglected for a long period, and then reviving it again. Latterly it has become very popular in riding, for which it is excellently qualified.

In undress it is impossible to dress a fine leg, more especially of a short person, to greater advantage than in a Hessian; and it must be allowed, where other requisites correspond, it adds a great deal of dignity and command to the person, setting off the figure to considerable advantage.

Hessians are a very expensive wear, and, like almost all other manufactures in the present day, may be superbly worked and finished, being bent and creased in the most exquisite manner, without ever losing shape. That kind of shape most admired, when pulled on the leg, should be high enough to let the tassel touch the knee-pan, and then be lowered to the calf, when the dents will form fuller and much handsomer than when contracted and held in, which latter way causes the boot to sit stiffly, and want that elastic spring in the leather that the method I point out possesses.

## THE TOP-BOOT

is almost entirely a sporting fashion, and boasts scarcely of any difference in make, with the exception of the top. Although they are worn by noblemen and gentlemen occasionally in hunting, they are in general use among the lowest orders, such as jockeys, grooms, butchers, &c.; I would, therefore, by no means advise them even for riding, except professionally for the prize cup, or at a hunting match. I do not know how it is, but notwithstanding the rank in society of thousands, who wear and patronise them, we are apt in London to connect something very low with their appearance. This style of boot when worn should only be with drab or white corded breeches. Spirits of vitriol mixed with a little fine powdered pipeclay, will be found an excellent cleaner of the tops, which should always be spotless.

## THE WELLINGTON,

together with the following, are the only boots in general wear; to be any thing like the fashion, they should have the toes at least an inch and a half square—such being the custom for both boots and shoes. Like the boots above mentioned, these are commonly made of calf-skin, though among the *ton*, for the sake of expense, doubtless, Spanish leather is used. This, I think, except in dress shoes, for which it only is qualified, should never be used; as it never possesses a quarter the jet brilliancy well-polished calf-skin can boast; while, in point of wear, it is far inferior.

## BLUCHERS AND COLLEGIANS

are a half-boot, one and the same, with this difference, that the former laps over the front and ties; whereas the other does not tie or lap over, but a piece is cut out from each side, which enables it to be pulled on by the tops before and behind.

These boots, for summer wear, while equal in appearance and durability with Wellingtons, are much more comfortable, confining the ancle less, and are so much easier put on. In price, too, they are much more economical, and equally fashionable in make; the only real difference between them and the Wellington is, that the latter takes more leather for the tops and lining, as well as additional work, which renders them much dearer.

## SHOES

can only be divided into two classes, long quarters and short quarters, that is dress and undress; the dress being generally termed pumps, and are always adopted in full evening costume, as being absolutely indispensable to *etiquette*. These should always be made of Spanish leather. In the present fashion, which is very well contrived for showing off the feet, the sides of the shoe should not be above an inch and a half high, and the leather not proceed above the same height over the toe; only, in fact, just sufficient to keep firmly on the foot. The tie should be of broad ribbon, made into a small double bow. Buckles are only used in the army, navy, and marines, and should be set with brilliants.

## DRESS BOOT-SHOE.

I have observed this boot under the denomination of dress, not of long invention, that is worthy of some notice under this head, and which certainly is an excellent substitute for dress shoes. I wish to be understood, I do not here mean ball-room dress, but dinner dress.

In the entire shape of a Wellington boot, uncovered by the trousers, they present the exact image of a shoe with the trousers over the instep. The stocking is effected by black cloth or India rubber in appearance, which is introduced under the sides and top of the leather part, resembling the shoe, as in the annexed figure.

This boot is invented, doubtless, for the mere purpose of saving trouble in dress; for without attending to silk stockings or the trouble of tying *bows*, you have merely to slip on the boots, and you are *featly* equipped in a moment. But the great advantage this boot offers to many I shall proceed to unfold. It is particularly applicable to those who wish to heighten their stature, a thing this will enable them to do in any degree that an undress boot will admit of, by having high heels. These can be two or even three inches if required; only two things should be observed: when they are very high, the aforesaid heels should be tipped with cork at least half an inch in thickness, so that no more reverberation need be made than with a pump to screen them completely from "human ken;" the trousers should be made very long, even to touching the ground, and strapped. Oh! what a transformation is here, my countrymen, in a diminutive man!

By these means, the most feasible possible, you have the advantage of appearing in full drawing-room dress with little trouble; and if undersized, with a very sensible improvement of stature, which, if followed in the manner my instructions have pointed out, cannot give the slightest cause to suspect you are actually walking upon *raisers*.

There are few purchases, perhaps, in which persons are more liable to be taken advantage of than in boots or shoes, for which purpose I shall proceed to give a little advice upon the subject.

### THE SOLES,

upon which great dependence ought to be placed, in boots should properly be composed of bull's hide, well tanned; whereas a spurious leather, not possessing half its durability, from the cow, is too frequently in use among the trade, more particularly wholesale country manufacturers, who supply town with ready-made boots and shoes, when it is passed off unsuspected, even as the best materials. When you want a pair of boots to wear well, never choose the thick-soled. Beware of them, most erudite reader; they are the most deceptious things in the world, like women, "made but to betray." I will explain. Hide, that is the best, should be about a quarter of an inch in thickness when it is cut up for soling; but previously to cutting out the precise shape required, it should be beaten as hard as a block until reduced to half its original thickness, when it is in a fit state to be pared and sewed. It will then, as a matter of course, wear well, if bull's hide; but the practice is as common as possible, for shoemakers to put on the hide, when indifferent in quality and will not bear beating, without the requisite form, when the unwary purchaser is too often taken in from judging by the thickness rather than the quality. Besides, when well beaten, independent of its superior wear, the sole receives a spring from it. How much neater, too, does it look, while it is effectual in excluding the wet, which the porous quality of the unbeaten hide in a short time admits. Indeed it may be considered as a rule almost unexceptionable, that you will never perceive good boots with thick soles, unless, indeed, they are double.

### NAILS,

I am convinced, without in any way injuring the appearance of a boot, are an immense saving. They should always be very small, and placed in with neatness and care, to be serviceable, and so as to counterbalance any inequalities in the wear. There has lately come up a patent nail, much commended; but, as I know nothing of it from experience, I cannot speak of its merit.

## UPPER LEATHERS.

The upper calf-skin leather of a boot, to be excellent, should be firm, strong, and rather waxy to the hand, and should not stretch or give way, but in a very trifling degree.

When you purchase boots or shoes, and desire good service from them, rub them well inside and out with sweet oil, then let them stand three or four days; when, after rubbing them well again with a warm dry flannel, you can wear them. By doing this, simple as it is, the upper leathers will wear nearly as long again in many cases; while, at the same time, it renders the leather soft and pliable to the feet, preventing corns, and ensures it perfectly waterproof.

*Names and Addresses of Shoemakers.*

W. Carter, No. 7, Southampton-street, Strand.
Bowtell, No. 49, Skinner-street, and 58, Cheapside.

TASTE

*in the selection of*

DRESS,

*and the want of it.*

# CHAPTER VII.

---

TALL AND SHORT MEN, AND FAIR AND DARK COMPLEXIONS,
SEPARATELY CONSIDERED.

DRESS, of course, in all its varieties, to look well, or set the person off to advantage, depends entirely upon the figure and complexion. I have endeavoured to delineate the different fashions and colours best calculated to win the eye of taste. I consider this requisite, the more particularly so, as those whom probably I now address have neither time, leisure, nor inclination, to take that proper observation and study upon the subject that are necessary. Indeed, the very great influence the power of dress has, though acknowledged by all, is by no means glanced at in its minutiæ; probably, in some degree, for the preceding reasons.

## TALL MEN,

whose figures on the average are of a spare habit, require mostly squareness and stoutness of exterior added to the figure, an ungainly slimness having a very imbecile appearance. The following advice will apply to them: the coat, which (except surtouts, well lined) should never be buttoned, should be padded under the arms, immediately below the pits, running down the sides, and tapering off at the waist; also, on the exterior of each shoulder. The chest, by this management, seems broader and more open; while the waist, by comparison, is rendered small, whereby the whole of the figure is very greatly improved. The make of the trousers should always be full, and worn without any straps. Shoes, and a low-crowned hat, should accompany this style of dress. Dark colours diminish the size as light magnify; the former should therefore be preferred. If the above be put in force, however thin the individual, a square set and open exterior may be obtained. It were as well, too, when the person chances to be very spare and lank, that the fronts of the coat on the chest receive a thorough military pad; the collar, too, should be very broad and rolling.

## SHORT MEN,

with very few exceptions, are desirous of improving their stature; nor are there, I think, any set of men, with defects in their appearance, who bear their lot with so ill a grace; though, by the way, they are commonly the most perfectly formed. Yet, for all this, none can seem more conscious that something is wanting; an elevation, in fact, which there are equally many would as gladly resign if possible.

It may, indeed, be remarked in common, how very upright a small man walks; how loud he talks, that he may be seen and heard; and all because he is fully determined not to allow his dignity to be overlooked on the score of his height, by his more elevated neighbours. These he always views with a jealous and suspicious eye. Again, what a fretful petulance is frequently discernible upon his countenance, under a number of different little circumstances, calculated to set his deficiency in glaring and mortifying colours before him. Such, for instance, as being obliged, by some unlucky movement, which his utmost vigilance could not have anticipated, to parade with some remarkably tall woman whose shoulders he scarcely reaches; then, being desired by some thoughtless *belle* to reach her fan or a book from some shelf which his most strenuous efforts, even with the aid of a jump now and then, will not allow him to accomplish. Oh, sad alternative! he is obliged to mount a chair like a child, with a satanic grin, as he presents the dearly-got article, almost ready to sink with shame and rage at the scarcely-to-be-suppressed laughter—who can tell?—perhaps from the very woman he fondly loves! Misery and madness are in the thought to a mind of sensibility. Did Count Browlinska, or Baba ever experience this exquisite torture?

Such, perhaps, is a slight, and not imperfect, sketch of some of the miseries endured by the little; who, while I admit them to be the most

talented and clever, frequently render them
selves ridiculous on this very account, without
any reason, as I shall display; for nothing, with
a little insight, is easier to remedy, by means of
high heels and the proper choice and kind of
colours in dress: the former of these influencing
it in reality, and the two latter only in appearance. As tall people are generally thin, on the
same estimate it will mostly be found that short
are inclining to be stout or fat. When this is
the case, I recommend the wearing of a band,
which should be worn with a tight-fitting coat
that sits well at the waist, and tight pantaloons
or trousers. The hat, of which, in a previous
part of this work I have stated the consequence,
should be high, small-crowned, and narrow-
rimmed. The coat, if in undress, should be a
short surtout, the trousers light-coloured; if in
summer, white—no other colour rendering the
stature so tall in appearance.

Now I compute—if a man 5 feet 4 inches thus
dressed, wear heels an inch and a-half, at three
or four yards distance he will appear 5 feet 8
inches; while at twenty yards he will seem a

tall man. So much for what may be done by a little attention.

The great distinction, as may be gleaned from the foregoing remarks, in bestowing that appearance of height, is greatly influenced by wearing a frock-coat, which should always be buttoned, and as short as possible, without looking singular. Then the tight-looking legs of course elongate the figure; the reason why I strenuously recommend Hessians, which, as I have before said, independent of all fashion, are generally the most becoming; and when any thing is so, without looking remarkable or conspicuous, it should always be adopted. For dinner dress, as I have previously observed, a friendly and excellent facility is afforded for the same advantage in company, which so immensely distinguishes a man when in undress.

## FAIR AND DARK COMPLEXIONS.

The appearance of the countenance is very greatly subjected to be relieved or depressed by the influence of colours. To be aware immediately of this fact, you have only to perceive how wretched white neckcloths make some people appear; those, for instance, of a sallow skin; while, on the opposite, a black velvet or satin stock throws, by its comparative depth of hue, the former into shade. All this is either more or less regulated by other colours. On dark people a dark coat looks best; black for the neck, most assuredly; then, as too much black would look gloomy, they should be relieved by a white or buff waistcoat.

The chief requisite in the countenance (as far as I have been enabled to trace this subject), to look well in a white or light cravat, is a clear complexion and bright eyes, which give the face an animated look; for I have remarked, that a dull or heavy expression of countenance, resulting from bile or other causes, natural or acquired, looks very miserable in light-coloured cravats; by these complexions nothing lighter than iron-gray should be worn.

You have only to walk the streets of London to perceive how little these facts are attended to, or not observed by the parties themselves. There is one great advantage attending fair men, thought not, perhaps, generally esteemed such favourites with the *fair sex* as the dark, they can assume almost all colours indiscriminately, with a few exceptions, without presenting much difference, other than the appearance of a change.

# CHAPTER VIII.

———

ON THE PERSON AND CARRIAGE;
WITH HINTS AND ADVICE

As I have observed in my Preface, dress, however handsome and fashionable, can never be becoming on any whose figure has contracted any of those defects or inelegancies which, on being traced to their origin, are generally found to proceed from some neglect during the probationary term of childhood. It is at this momentous period of life, when the body should be tended as well as the mind, lest the one, like the other in evil, "grow with their growth," until too late, perhaps, for remedy. However, with determination and a full sense of the misfortune attending those grown up with a perverted figure or carriage, they may, in course of time, by perseverance, be overcome.

To a mind of sensibility, what a blessing must this be, in getting rid of that which is an eyesore to others, and a subject of common remark among our acquaintances. It certainly should be a sufficient *impetus* to the mind, to dislodge an enemy so formidable in itself.

In society there is no outward quality so pleasing to the sight, as ease and grace of carriage, without any distortion or twist of the frame into positions never intended by nature; and, on the contrary, there is nothing will form a more ready or mirthful satire for the young and the beautiful of the other sex, than evident want of this acquirement. It is even painful to perceive it. How imposing, manly, and majestic, is the walk of some men, contrasted with the scrambling shuffle of others, even though the first be far inferior in nature's advantages; yet how infinitely superior will this advantage alone make him over those who scarce would be noticed. There seems, in fact, in a measured and easy step, slow or quick, all that self-possession in mind and person which the latter looks so miserably without. There are men, indeed—to such a lamentable deficiency is this carried—who, though perhaps not above one or two and twenty, might, from their bent figure, at some little distance, be taken positively for old men:—how shocking to the eye! To obtain that desirable requisition, a good walk, I cannot but deem it necessary to recommend to those deficient in this respect a fatiguing drill twice a week under a drill-sergeant, which, if kept up perseveringly for any length of time, will cure any contraction or twist of the person acquired through early negligence.

A good figure—and it is in the power of all in some degree to improve this most important particular—should possess the following qualifications. The neck should be tolerably long, with suitable muscle in thickness, curving rather slopingly down to the shoulders, in proportion, about one-third the decline a woman's should possess. The chest, upon which the whole body hinges, should be broad and extended in front, throwing the shoulders and arms behind, the latter of which should hang with a gentle curve from the elbow down the sides. The legs, which should be regulated by the body, will then support the body easy and unconstrained; while the toes of the feet, to which I would particularly direct the observance of my reader, should always be turned inclining out.

In making these few preceding remarks, I would by no means have any to suppose that my attention is particularly bordering on the military; by no means; though I would have every gentleman tread the ground as an officer should; that is, without affectation, easy, and erect, with a frank and open front. The difference alone that ought to exist *outwardly*, should be uniform, for why, I say, is the one alone to have a desirable advantage which the other, by a little study, may also possess himself of.

There is no exercise, I think, more conducive to improve the figure and carriage than fencing: for this reason alone it should be acquired. It tends greatly to open the chest, consequently flattens the back, and, by gracefully calling the muscles and joints into measured play, ensures, as much as any exercise can do, excellent health. The attention, indeed, that is so particularly paid to the person and carriage in learning this accomplishment, must, as a matter of course, greatly improve them.

Of a great number of the gymnastic exercises introduced by Professor Voelker, and lately so very popular, I very greatly disapprove, upon the principle that, though I acknowledge they may greatly strengthen the body, at the same time they are apt to strain and distort the joints of youth. When the person is set, this is otherwise.

I shall now speak of the defects too frequently incident to the carriage, which long experience on the subject enables me to advise with the utmost confidence. Defects generally consist under the following names:—the stoop, the lob-side, turning in the toes, and sprawling of the arms.

The stoop, while it lessens the height, and presents aged deformity to the eye, is equally prejudicial to health, as it contracts the chest, which, as a reference to medical advice will inform the intelligent reader, is very often the sole cause of consumption or decline. To recover from this degrading innovation on the form, the dumb-bells should be constantly exercised each morning; if the case be very bad, at least two hours—and persevered in until they form that elevation originally intended by nature.

This kind of exercise, to be rendered beneficial, should be thus conducted. The bells, which should weigh from five to nine pounds the pair, according to the strength of the individual, should meet with a measured stroke behind the back, the arms being nearly stiffly extended when striking. The head and neck, too, upon which the efficacy of this treatment depends, being all the while thrown back as far as possible. The rest of the body should be quite straight, as in the first position. The lob-side, or slouching gait, is one which, like the former, is chiefly prevalent among tall people, and consists in walking more on one side than the other, which has a very crooked and unpleasant appearance. It is too frequently accompanied by a violent swinging of the arms, which, as if indignant at being allied to so contracted a body, seem as if about to quit their owner at short notice. To destroy this habit requires much attention; it should be effected by carrying a weight from twenty to thirty pounds, depending from the arm on that side where the twist is. This should be carried walking to and fro in a long room or garden, as long as the exercise can be borne, which will not exceed an hour each morning. By continuing in this, gradually the contracted side will assume its pristine place by the constant pull of the weight.

Turning the toes in! What does this not bear in indubitable evidence? That he has never learned to dance, therefore unfitted to enter a ball-room, or, in fact, any room, where the refined and elegant are admitted.

To cure this awkward and ungainly habit, it is merely requisite to practise the position of standing upright, closing the legs, and turning out the toes till they form a straight line, the heels at the same time touching. It will be found easy in beginning, to practise this exercise against the walls of a room, or a chair, until you are sufficiently initiated into the art to form the position without assistance.

I now have to recur to a fault which many persons have, otherwise, perhaps, possessing a very tolerable carriage; this is a sprawling of the arms, if I may so use the term, which it would frequently seem were appendages that might be done without, as is proved by a number of little fidgety expedients, apparently almost unconsciously resorted to, to get their intruders out of the way; such, for instance, as thrusting them behind, or pushing the hands into the trousers' pockets, or elevating them with clasped hands over the head, as if despairing of ever finding what they seem so much in quest of, a resting-place.

Carrying weights in the hands may be of some service, though, unless the energies of the mind be called in, I despair of their eradicating this last silly habit.

To walk well, which I think is totally independent of dancing, the body should be perfectly straight, easy, and free in its motions:

the soles of the feet should be placed flat on the ground, at once keeping uniform time.

There should, in fact, be no kind of embarrassment in one who attains a prepossessing carriage; and though the dancing-master can doubtless affect a great deal in drilling the legs, the head and chest among very admirable dancers, I am sorry to observe, are often much neglected. For general drill, indeed, it will be found, that the fencing-master must be allowed supremacy, as the motions of every limb, together with the eye, come under a close and severe scrutiny.

# CHAPTER IX.

———

## ON UNIFORM AND MASQUERADE DRESS.

UNIFORM, which marks in itself a difference or similarity of habits, is a distinction common to all the nations in the world; even the most barbarous of the Indian and Lapland tribes possessing some outward distinguishing peculiarity from each other in dress and arms. In Europe, however, this habit is more particularly worn to denote the honourable profession of arms, which in the army is known by the more proper appellation of regimentals. To do this subject any thing like justice, would be to fill many volumes such as this; our notice, therefore, must be somewhat brief, even in a general view of

what touches so many nations. From these
I shall select the most prominent for pictur-
esqueness and beauty.

The richest and most splendid uniforms
perhaps any where, are worn by the Turks, to
whom their style of dress is becoming in the
first degree. When they are mounted on horse-
back, the figure, singly according with that
of the charger, from its trappings, has a very
muscular and powerful appearance, notwithstanding their known remarkable activity, which
renders them as light cavalry, even equal to the
Cossacks. The crescented turban, crimson vest
and sash, together with the long loose flowing
trousers and bright Mocassin, presenting a novel
sight to the unpractised eye. This is greatly
enhanced by the martial and free bearing of the
men, and the glitter of their superbly mounted
and wrought arms. These in Turkey seem to
occupy the greatest care in their outward deco-
rations, gold and silver chased mounting even
being common among the private soldiery.—
Among their officers and chiefs, no description
can exceed the splendour of their arms, being

frequently set with jewels of immense value. These generally consist of a sabre (of a chief), a case of ataghans or poniards, and a brace of pistols. Their sabres, which are celebrated throughout the world for their beautiful temper, being manufactured at Damascus, as well as their long curved blades, which are generally inlaid with gold, displaying great ingenuity of workmanship. The ataghan, which is worn at all periods, is always very richly mounted. Their fire-arms, however beautiful in their exterior, are far inferior to European manufacture in use.

There is, indeed, altogether a wild and picturesque appearance about the Turkish military which affords a very singular relief to English or French uniform.

Of the French, perhaps, to pay them a just compliment, they are distinguished for their taste and judgment in selection of uniforms, as their army can witness, while they have been copied, in some degree, by almost all the nations around them; among whom I am sorry to name England. The *Garde Nationale* and *Garde Royale* present a very splendid appearance, as well as some of the carabinier regiments.

One singularity attending most French cavalry uniforms is, the troopers are mounted with two different colours, one down the sides and the other in the inner side of the legs. But this latter peculiar fashion is now common among some of the Prussian and Austrian heavy cavalry.

With regard to the Russian, Prussian, German, and Austrian armies, there is little difference generally in regard to their fashions, the same colours and facings being very common among them in their different styles of dress. One singular difference only that strikes me at this moment, when contrasted with the English uniform, is the adoption of entire white for uniform among some crack regiments of Prussian and Austrian infantry, which render the regiments dressed in it remarkably fine-looking.

The uniforms of the united service of Great Britain display, perhaps, in their various specimens at the present period, probably the handsomest and most martial-looking in the world, except the French, whose troops, candour obliges me to say, may vie *in appearance* with us. Where can there be more splendid-looking uniforms than some of our dragoons wear. Witness the 7th, 8th, and 10th regiments of Hussars; last, and by no means *least*, the Guards, horse and foot.

The uniform and arrangement, indeed, of arms and furniture in the Life-Guards, presents a picture of what human ingenuity can invent: the arrangement is so admirable. For this, however, we are greatly indebted to the Germans, some of whose heavy armed cavalry may safely be termed equal to any in the world.

Cavalry has always been celebrated over the infantry for its advantages in screening and new fronting a bad figure; a reason why the younger branches of noble families, intended for the army, when possessing an indifferent exterior, always go into it. There an insignificant head is hidden under a martial plumed helmet: the coat, padded well in every direction, to sit perfect, while it is rendered small at the waist

by the use of stays—or a belt, as the former
term should never be uttered in ears polite.
Then as for bandy-legs, or knock-knees, they
are totally unseen in long, stiff, leathern boots,
that extend up on the thigh, to which two-inch
heels may be very safely appended; so that with
the cuirass and different accoutrement-straps,
it offers an effectual screen.

Now, not one-half of this can be effected
in the infantry; marching from thirty to forty
miles in the day, with high heels, would be its
own punishment. Some of our foot uniforms
are singularly martial and striking to the
eyes of foreigners, such for instance as our
Highland regiments and rifle brigades; the
latter, on account of its gloomy simplicity in
point of colour.

Of navy uniforms—a truly great change
may be said to have taken place for the better
in these since the last regulation made by the
Board of Admiralty, while the distinctions of
rank in the service are rendered more clear and
becoming. The gold-lace bands down the sides
supplant the white cloth lately in use with a

much handsomer effect. The introduction of frock-coats too, in undress, is decidedly a refinement, which, with the abolition of the dirk, placed the junior class of officers, as volunteers and midshipmen, on a more equal and proper footing, in respect to outward appearance.

Of masquerade dresses, to which I would now call the attention of my reader, I shall take a review, as far as my contracted pages will admit, on the subject.

The carnival, as it is called, at Venice, is there, perhaps, one of the gayest and most amusing sights an Englishman can well conceive, lasting for six weeks together. During this period all seem turned to a new life; young and old, rich and poor, turning into the grand square of St. Mark. The illuminations, music, laugh, song, or dance, among the wild and motley-looking groups, with the more immediate vagaries of *Arlechino*, and *Poleinello*, with their satellites *Il Pantaleau, Il Dottore Graziano*, and *Scaramouche*, are sufficient to please and force the laugh from the sedatest. There is, too, a lively turn of wit and repartee banded about, with a grace and fascination among the lowest, that by no means affords a favourable comparison to the English. The French (who come next the Italian, in their accomplishment at these scenic reviews,) render it an amusement to which they are particularly partial; it is therefore very popular, the two sexes mixing almost indiscriminately in it. To render, however, masquerades amusing requires a natural sprightliness of wit and manners, with great shrewdness and knowledge of the character assumed. It is the possession of these particulars, with a wonderful flow of animal spirits, that renders our foreign neighbours so capable of giving effect to masquerades. In England, I am sorry to say, from what I have witnessed of this amusement, I have seen it degenerate into mere solemn nonsense, or low and obscene mirth, however handsome the dresses may have been. This unfavourable comparison, indeed, may easily be accounted for. Notwithstanding the natural *gaieté de cœur* of the Italian and French, it may truly be said to form part of their education from early childhood. In

England it is almost entirely neglected. Among the higher orders it is very seldom indulged in, except in the form of a fancy-dress ball, which is truly elegant, when the dresses are well chosen. Neither is it attended with the incessant noise of many voices, or the squabbles that invariably take place in the best-regulated meetings of this former sort.

For those possessed of tolerably good figures and countenances, who are fond of a *figurative* display, I name the following characters:

| *Characters.* | *Names of Plays.* |
| --- | --- |
| Romeo. | Romeo and Juliet. |
| Bertram. | Bertram. |
| The Vampire. | The Vampire. |
| Macbeth. | Macbeth. |
| Robin Hood. | Old Character. |
| Charles the Second. | Charles the Second. |
| Villiers, Duke of Buckingham. | ditto. |
| Charles XII. of Sweden. | Charles the XII. |
| Vanderdecken. | The Flying Dutchman. |
| Don Juan. | Old Character. |

Any thing like a detail of the different dresses would be to occupy a space allotted to other and more important matter, and at the same time both tedious and useless, inasmuch as the reference I have named under this head will bestow, I am convinced, general satisfaction in those particulars, whether as regards purchase or hire.

For those fond of the comic, or laughable line, I set down the following original and amusing characters so well known:

Jeremy Diddler.
Shacabac.
Jemmy Green.
Apothecary in Romeo and Juliet.
Baron Munchausen.
Leporello.
A Counsellor.
Harlequin.
Clown.
Pantaloon, &c.

Soldiers, when they are intended to be represented, should mostly, for the sake of novelty, be in foreign uniforms, and that, too, correctly; for which purpose a reference to *Bell's Gentleman's Magazine* would be as well.

I have, in a previous article, urged the necessity of possessing a good carriage in assuming fancy dress: it is indeed absolutely requisite to receive any eclat.

Of certain kinds of horrible nondescript characters I have, generally speaking, a poor opinion, though they do well enough to fill up a group;—Indians and savages, from all quarters of the earth the same. Caliban, in the Tempest, is the only thorough excellent character I would advise to be supported in the *low horribles*; not but that Robbers, Monks, and Foresters are very good old English characters to support.

Nautical characters, as men-of-war's men, smugglers, pirates, and Thames watermen in London, are very popular and amusing characters in London (*vide* minors, Surrey and Coburg).

A man-of-war's-man at masquerades is very seldom well sustained. T. P. Cooke is decidedly the best I have ever seen or can conceive on a stage; and to ensure the utmost advantage in dress, his need only be copied. Smugglers should be dressed generally with blood-red caps, or blue or red striped, if preferred; a Guernsey frock, and high boots.

*Pirates ad libitum* almost, so the nautical character be in any way preserved. Finally, with respect to arms of whatsoever description, when they are worn, they should always be bright, handsome, and showy; nothing, I think, having so wretched an appearance as rusty blades and barrels. Oh, 'tis rank! it smells so of marine stores.

Simmonds, No. 13, Holywell-street, Strand.

# CHAPTER X.

―――――

## THE TOILETTE,

### WITH HINTS AND RECIPES.

It has frequently been a matter of opinion and argument, which should claim the preference in the human construction, face or figure, either advocate producing very excellent reasons in support of each opinion. Whether the face, indeed, be of more importance or no than the figure, is a question I by no means intend to agitate. Suffice it, it should at all events be sufficient to claim that attention, both as regards health and appearance, it is my present purpose to pay it. In the ensuing pages, in which the appearance is so very materially concerned, I purpose confining myself entirely

to the following component parts of my subjects:—The skin and hands, the hair, and lastly,
the teeth, all of which stand so much in need
of our care.

## THE SKIN AND HANDS.

The skin, which depresses or adds so much to
the look of health in the appearance, though it
may depend so much upon a number of causes
resulting from nature, is, without doubt, very
greatly affected by the outward treatment. This,
with the eye, are the almost sole regulators of
health in appearance; too generally, however,
misinterpreted in consumptions. Bad complexions, though they may frequently be natural to
the constitution, proceeding from a variety of
causes, as bile, scurvy, &c., I am persuaded they
as often result from nothing else but improper
outward treatment. This outward treatment I
speak of chiefly comprehends the method of
washing, kind of water and soap, &c., which
has a greater influence than is commonly known
on the subject.

I set it down for a rule myself, and therefore recommend it to the notice of others, to wash both summer and winter in warm water; its advantages to the discerning should be obvious, in its efficacy in opening the pores of the skin, which is softened, refreshed, and refined by its application, while those small secretions of imperceptible humours that gather on the surface are always dispersed. In winter, indeed, it is the only way of thoroughly cleansing the skin. I myself have never more particularly felt the benefit of washing well in warm water, than on a long march or a field-day, when, however violent the exercise or fatigue, I have always felt a degree of comfort I ascribe solely to the use of warm water, while I have experienced just the contrary feeling when there have been times when I have not been enabled to procure this luxury. With regard to soap, I think as much, if not more, depends upon it than water; still, such singular opinions do prevail in this age of wonders, that I have known the common-est yellow soap preferred for the complexion. This is downright folly, potash and spirits of

turpentine would poison a pig. If a skin dry
and shining, like polished brass, be desired, a
few weeks' unremitting practice will bestow it
in perfection. Setting aside the fulsome method
of puffing so much practised in the present day,
that so frequently purchases a name for unwor-
thy articles, there are no soaps so excellent as
those of the Windsor kind. Brown I prefer. For
those, however, who have rough skins, if there
be any outward application that can be efficacious, it is the use of fine Scotch oatmeal, which
possesses a peculiar property of whitening the
skin and rendering it very soft, whether face or
hands; the reasons why it is held in great estimation by so many of the fair sex. But it should
never be used until you have well washed with
soap, when it requires a little fresh warm water,
and should then be sprinkled on the towel and
rubbed on, after which it should be well washed
off again. This, and I particularly speak from
my own experience and that of many friends
who have, like myself, used it for the hands,
by degrees will make them change their colour,
until they have that appearance a gentleman's

hand should possess. In fact, I have known people of very excellent family and fortune, who at first sight have been stamped as low society, by the unprepossessing appearance of their hands.

With regard to the practice of recovering the appearance of the hands by using oil and wax melted together, rubbed over the hands, and covering them with kid gloves, though this will certainly improve the skin, it is extremely prejudicial to health, as it prevents the free circulation of the blood.

Of the nails, which form the most important portion of the hand, and upon the excellence of which it greatly depends, they should frequently, if thin, be scraped until they obtain a sufficient thickness. This paring, which should be evenly performed, likewise gives them a good colour and gloss, which they should always possess. Filbert-nails are the most approved for beauty, but it only needs perseverance to obtain this kind of shape, by constantly, after the hands have been well washed in hot water, and the nails well brushed, turning the skin that skirts them back with the towel, which should become a habit, when the nail will appear much longer, and more filbert-like than it would otherwise have done. This skin, of such consequence to the nail and hand generally, should never be cut, as it is only a provocative for stronger growth.

## THE HAIR.

Of the hair, which has such capabilities for setting off the most indifferent countenance, the importance that is attached to it sufficiently marks the proper estimation it is held in.

The chief attributes of hair should be curl, strength, and gloss. All three of which, however sparing nature may have been in her gifts, art can make up. Hair, which in itself depends for nourishment upon the head, when refused that requisite supply by a dry habit of body, and turns of deadish hue, should be oiled every morning. The way to apply oils or grease of any kind to nourish the hair, is to rub it well in at the roots, when its essential virtue can only be of service, and then brush it well. Brushing is as absolutely required by the hair, as washing by the face, it is this that bestows that fine gloss which so much improves the appearance of the hair, at the same time excluding all dandriff. This ever forms and renders the hair of a dead and unanimated appearance, when not well brushed. A hard penetrating, and a soft brush should be alternately used. The former strengthens the roots of the hair by impelling a brisker circulation of the blood, while the latter bestows the shine or polish.

Oils in general, I am by no means partial to. There are, indeed, scarcely any, besides the Macassar, upon which much reliance should be placed. Bears' grease, when genuine, there can be no doubt, is very nourishing to the hair, and greatly promotes its growth, as well as strength. But neither oil nor bears' grease should be applied to the hair without a good brushing. In fact, if rubbed softly on the top of the brush, and so applied, it is quite as well. The hair should never be suffered to grow long uncut, as it seems to fade and droop, and the ends split;

for this reason, to have it in perfection, it should be trimmed at the least once every month. I likewise recommend washing it once a fortnight in the summer, and half as often in winter. This should be done with water, hot as you can bear it; and if soap be used in winter, in summer it never should. Care should be taken in washing it well out, as it is pernicious in the extreme.

The following recipe for making an economical beautifier of the hair, I am indebted to a friend for, and as I have had so long a tried proof of its virtue, I can with pleasure impart it to others.

### RECIPE FOR THE HAIR.

Of fine Beef Marrow take 1/4 lb.
Of Burnt Brandy two table spoonfuls.
With the same quantity of the best Flask Oil.

These should be mixed and allowed to simmer over the fire, when it should constantly be skimmed until it boil; when, after boiling a little time, the perfume bergamot, musk, lavender, or rose, as preferred, should be added, when it should be potted and tied up. This, if properly managed, will keep any time, and will be found to impart a beautiful freshness to the hair.

## THE TEETH.

Finally, I shall now take the teeth into consideration. The value of these must, I think, be too well known to need much urging on the subject, considering the estimation they are held in by the young and handsome of both sexes. Neglect of these important organs to the human frame is most lamentably felt and deplored by those who have been guilty of it, as no portion of humanity decays so soon as these. At all times inspiring loathing and disgust when rotten or soiled, teeth, when they are white, even, and firm, are a great beauty and blessing every one ought to feel conscious of. If a man but possess, indeed, this one solitary advantage in personal appearance, it is certainly a great advocate among the angels of this lower world, it being a truly considerable saving clause.

To ensure sound teeth to a good old age, it is absolutely proper to begin from early youth by cleaning them regularly every morning. The durability of teeth depends upon the thickness of the enamel, which should never be rubbed too long with powder of any sort, as the constant repetition of it very sensibly wears it, which will grow thin and be rendered unable of long withstanding the relentless corroding influence of time.

The teeth, which consume more by night than by day, should be rinsed well with water and a soft brush previous to going to bed. This disperses the vegetable and animal matter that after meals is apt to get into the interstices of the teeth, and there corrupts; which, though not felt then, gradually lays the foundation of decay.

However nauseous and unpleasant it may be to the palate, I am convinced there is nothing that preserves the teeth so well as tobacco. The reason why you will never see an old or inveterate smoker with bad teeth. On this account I recommend the ashes of tobacco, mixed with a little salt and fine charcoal, as the best preservative for the teeth: of the vegetable acids that are vended, and so much commended as toothpowders, though they, like every other acid, will produce a whiteness on the first application, it never remains, not even for an hour, while its influence is most pernicious, implanting the seeds of decay in a very short time. Finally, to conclude with respect generally to imperfections in the teeth and gums, timely recourse should always be had to a dentist, who, by judicious management, may afford a remedy which is so frequently essentially necessary for the preservation of these important organs.

*Names and Addresses of Perfumers.*

Rowland and Son, No. 20, Hatton-garden.
Dick, No. 194, Bishopsgate-street.

THE END.